Urban Food Webs

Building Resilient and Sustainable Cities

Table of Contents

Chapter 1. Introduction

In this special report, we delve into the compelling universe of Urban Food Webs, an emerging field blending sustainability, community dynamics, and urban living to forge resilient cities of the future. As city-dwellers bear witness to escalating environmental concerns, this timely report explores innovative ways to create more robust and sustainable urban ecosystems. More than just another urban planning document, this exciting and eye-opening report uncovers how cities can progress towards self-sustaining models, where local food production and city life intertwine in harmonious balance. Proceed with us on this invigorating journey, because by understanding and implementing Urban Food Webs, you may be part of transforming your city into a resilient, green future, contributing not just to personal wellness, but our planet's health as well. This is more than just an investment in knowledge; it's an investment in our collective future.

Chapter 2. Understanding Urban Food Webs: Basics and Beyond

Urban food webs represent a burgeoning area of study combining aspects of ecology, urban planning, and community development to create sustainable, resilient urban ecosystems. By understanding their underpinnings, their potential, and how to effectively cultivate them, we unveil an exciting path towards a more sustainable future where cities are not just consumers, but also producers of their own food and other crucial resources.

2.1. A Primer on Food Webs

Food webs illustrate the complex network of energy flow through an ecosystem. They revolve around who eats whom, starting with sunlight and plants, flowing through herbivores to apex predators, and unwinding through decomposers recycling energy back into the ecosystem. The energy transfer from each trophic level is integral to all life forms in the ecosystem.

However, in our current urban environments, the food web is primarily linear and unidirectional, following a factory-to-consumer model driven by widespread importation. Urban food webs aim to refashion these linear chains into intricate, more natural and cyclical webs, channeling increased sustainability and autonomy within urban spaces.

2.2. The Urban Food Web: A New Paradigm

The urban food web concept seeks to nurture holistic, self-sustaining ecosystems within city environments. It involves collaboration across different sectors, engaging urban planners, horticulturists, community leaders, and citizens alike. The goal is to foster the presence of multiple, interdependent trophic levels within cities, thereby emulating a natural ecosystem and its energy flow.

The urban food web model not only enhances a city's food security but also benefits the environment significantly. It facilitates efficient resource utilization through local production and circulation, reducing carbon footprint and waste generation.

2.3. Dynamics of the Urban Food Web

Understanding the intricacies of the urban food web begins with interpreting its four core components: production, consumption, decomposing, and recycling.

1. Production: Planting urban gardens and developing urban farms for local crop production. Ideally, cities should allow diverse urban plant life not only confined to farmlands or allotted green spaces, but dispersed throughout the city, reflecting the rich biodiversity of a natural ecosystem.

2. Consumption: This involves citizens consuming locally produced food. Depending on the scale and intent, it could range from families eating produce from their own backyard gardens, to schools providing meals harvested from local urban farms.

3. Decomposition: Vital to the circular nature of food webs, decomposition recycles organic materials back into soil,

enriching it for higher quality plant growth. Decomposition can take shape through composting initiatives, worm farming, or other forms of organic waste recycling.

4. Recycling: Hand in hand with decomposition, the recycling component involves converting the decomposed organic materials back into nutrient-rich soil, completing the food web cycle and feeding back into production.

Understanding and implementing each stage successfully forms the core of a robust urban food web.

2.4. Moving Beyond Basics: Cultivating Urban Food Webs

Developing an efficient, productive urban food web requires careful planning, community engagement, and adaptive problem-solving. It also involves promoting biodiversity, ensuring equitable access to land and resources, creating opportunities for local trade, and encouraging public participation.

1. Promoting Biodiversity: Plant and animal biodiversity form the backbone of thriving food webs. Planting a variety of native species can attract wildlife, support pollinators, and improve the resiliency of local food systems against pests and diseases.

2. Access to Land and Resources: Equitable access to land and resources is crucial for cultivating an urban food web. City regulations should favour green space allocation for food production activities, encouraging community gardens, rooftop farming, and other urban agricultural practices.

3. Opportunities for Local Trade: Establishing farmers markets and community-supported agriculture can stimulate local economies and foster community interconnectedness, a crucial link within the urban food web.

4. Encouraging Public Participation: Ultimately, an urban food web can only thrive with robust community involvement. Encourage participation through educational programs, policy incentives, and community outreach, weaving the urban food web into the cultural fabric of the city.

2.5. Conclusion: The Resilient Urban Future

An effective urban food web mirrors the complex and cyclical nature of natural ecosystems, encouraging cities to produce, consume, decompose, and recycle locally, thereby fostering a resilient and sustainable urban environment. As we grapple with the realities of a changing climate and escalating urbanization, urban food webs offer a vital strategy to transition towards a greener, healthier, and more equitable future. It is not just a theoretical concept but a practical, achievable model that benefits urban dwellers, the broader community, and our planet at large. Understanding and implementing these intricate webs could well be the key to revitalizing our urban lands and securing our collective future.

Chapter 3. The Science of Sustainability: Urban Agriculture

In the quest for more sustainable cities, urban agriculture has emerged as a potential solution. It combines the principles of ecology, public health, and city planning in a way that can produce both healthy food and healthy communities. But what does it mean to be an effective urban farmer? Is it possible to cultivate thriving agricultural systems in the heart of the city? These questions and more form the core of what we now consider as the science of urban agriculture.

3.1. Challenges of Urban Agriculture

Urban farming, by nature, has to deal with some unique challenges. Land availability is often at a premium in cities. Farms need to be small, compact, and efficient to make the most of the available space. Urban soils may be contaminated with industrial pollutants, creating additional hurdles for healthy crop growth.

Water usage is a key concern in urban areas, where competition for water resources is high between various stakeholders. Moreover, city dwellers typically lack the agricultural skillset. Overcoming these obstacles requires innovative thinking and solutions that can be applied on a community level.

3.2. Innovative Farming Techniques

To confront these challenges, scientists and urban farmers are working together to devise novel cultivation techniques. Examples of these include vertical farming, hydroponics, aeroponics, and aquaponics.

Vertical farming involves growing crops in vertically stacked layers, usually inside buildings or containers. This multiplies the productive capacity of a given land area, enabling farmers to cultivate crops on a commercial scale in urban environments.

Hydroponics is a soil-less form of agriculture that uses mineral nutrient solutions in water, while aeroponics uses mist rather than a liquid medium. These techniques save water, prevent soil-borne diseases, and allow for precision control of nutrient supply.

Aquaponics is a particularly fascinating innovation. It is a system that combines fish farming (aquaculture) with hydroponics. The waste from the fish provides nutrients for the plants, and the plants clean the water for the fish—a neatly self-sustaining cycle.

3.3. The Role of Tech in Urban Farming

Technology plays a crucial role in increasing the efficiency and effectiveness of urban farming. Precision farming technologies allow urban farmers to monitor and adjust the conditions of their crops in real time – providing exactly the right amount of water, light, and nutrients each plant requires.

Robotics and automated systems are becoming increasingly prevalent in urban farming contexts. These tools can automate routine tasks like seeding, watering, and harvesting, thereby reducing labor costs and physical strain on the farmers.

3.4. The Public Health Perspective

Urban agriculture isn't just about food production. It's also about public health. Access to fresh, locally-produced foods can dramatically improve nutrition in urban areas, particularly in low-income neighborhoods which are often food deserts - areas without ready access to fresh, healthy, and affordable food.

The act of farming also has health benefits. It's physically active work, promoting exercise in an age of increasing sedentary lifestyles. It fosters a sense of community among urban dwellers, promoting mental wellbeing.

3.5. The outlook of Urban Agriculture

The future looks bright for urban agriculture. There is a growing recognition of its many benefits, from carbon sequestration to waste recycling, food security to community building, and this is prompting municipalities worldwide to integrate it into their urban development strategies.

Every city has its own unique opportunities and constraints, so there is no one-size-fits-all model for urban farming. But with the right blend of innovative thinking, community engagement, and science-based planning, urban farms can contribute significantly towards the goal of building more resilient, sustainable cities.

In conclusion, urban agriculture holds the potential to address multiple challenges of the urban environment, including food insecurity, archaic waste management systems, and ecological degradation. It reinstates communities as key stakeholders in securing their food needs and empowers city-dwellers to understand and appreciate the food system that sustains them. As we continue unfolding the vast potential of urban food webs and developing more resilient cities, the practice, implementation, and success of urban farming will indisputably be a major player.

Hence, anyone invested in the vision of sustainable cities of the future should consider urban agriculture not just a trend, but an integral part of urban life and a solution to many of our environmental and societal challenges. As we learn more about this exciting aspect of urban ecology, we'll understand better the prospects it holds for us, our communities, and our planet.

The science of sustainability is a multifaceted discipline, but with urban agriculture as one of its main components, we're stepping into a greener, healthier, and more equitable future - one plant, one neighborhood, one city at a time.

Chapter 4. Local Food Systems: A Closer Look

The global food supply chain is lengthy and complex, running from producers to consumers and encompassing multiple stakeholders in between. It's often depicted as a linear pathway, but the reality is far more complicated — more like a web than a single thread linking two points.

Many people aren't aware of this web in their own cities. Often, our food comes from places we can't pinpoint on a map; grapes from Chile, coffee from Ethiopia, or salmon from Alaska. While globalized food systems have certainly brought a variety of benefits, they've also grown increasingly precarious, beset by environmental decay, socio-economic disparity, and resilience challenges in the face of global shocks such as the COVID-19 outbreak. This has stirred conversations about enhancing the sustainability and robustness of our food systems — and at the center of this discourse is the reimagining of 'Local Food Systems.'

4.1. Defining Local Food Systems

The term "local food systems" refers to interconnected food production and distribution systems where foods are grown, processed, packaged, and consumed within a particular geographic boundary — say a county, a state, or in the case of urban areas, a city district.

Local food systems are based on small-scale agricultural practices that reduce the physical and temporal distance between food producers and consumers. They encompass a variety of models: community gardens, urban farms, farmer markets, food co-operatives, and community-supported agriculture (CSAs), to name a few.

Harnessing the power of local food systems involves rethinking our city landscapes and transforming underutilized spaces — rooftops, vacant lots, underused parks, and vertical facades — into productive green spaces. It's about connecting city dwellers with farming, fostering community links, and creating resilient cities by promoting local food security.

4.2. Benefits of Local Food Systems

Local food systems shrink food miles — the distance food travels from the field to the table — and this has significant environmental implications. First, it reduces carbon emissions linked to transportation. Secondly, local systems encourage biodiversity and sustainable farming practices, such as permaculture and organic farming, which is beneficial for soil health and local ecology.

From an economic perspective, local food systems stimulate local economies by keeping money circulating within the community, creating jobs from farming to processing and retailing.

Socio-culturally, local food systems help strengthen food literacy and promote healthier dietary choices. They bring communities together, fostering a sense of place and pride in local food production. They may also serve as tools for education and empowerment, allowing communities a more direct role in their own food security and fostering a greater understanding of food production.

4.3. Challenges Encountered in Local Food Systems

Even with these clear benefits, local food systems are not without challenges. For instance, urban farming may face zoning and land use issues. Moreover, seasonality can limit the availability of certain foods, and small-scale farming might not meet the entire food demand of growing urban populations.

Price is another tension point. Local, organic food can be more costly than imported goods, making it less accessible to parts of the community. These challenges raise questions about the equity and inclusivity of local food systems, and stress the need for supportive policies that ensure local food for all.

4.4. The Role of Innovation in Local Food Systems

Innovations in agricultural technology, such as vertical farming and hydroponics, offer promising solutions to some of these challenges. For instance, vertical farming allows cities to grow food year-round, regardless of their climate, while hydroponic systems offer highly-efficient ways of growing food in confined spaces, using less water and no soil — ideal for urban areas.

Digital technologies have also transformed local food systems. Platforms connecting farmers and consumers directly, online marketplaces for local food, urban farming apps, and digital traceability tools are paving the way for more resilient, sustainable and inclusive local food networks.

4.5. In Conclusion

In an era of escalating environmental crises and increasing urbanization, local food systems offer a critical avenue for cities to become more sustainable, resilient and inclusive. However, realizing their full potential will require addressing barriers, acknowledging complexities and capitalizing on innovative solutions. In other words, transforming our cities into robust food webs is not just about farming; it's about comprehensive urban planning, tech innovation, community participation, and equitable policymaking. Creating a local food system is a complex undertaking, but the benefits — a greener, healthier, and more resilient city — are immeasurable.

In the end, local food systems are more than just about food; they're about people, our cities, and fundamentally, our planet's future. As influencers of our urban landscapes, we may not all be farmers, but we are all stakeholders in our local food systems. As such, by understanding and supporting these systems, we are investing in our collective future. Dive deeper, ask questions, and remember — every bite you take, every decision you make, helps shape the food web of your city, and the world.

Chapter 5. From Concrete to Cultivation: Urban Agriculture Case Studies

The transformation from sprawling concrete jungles to green cultivations centers in cities around the globe has gained noticeable momentum in recent years. In this context, several pioneering urban farming initiatives effectively embraced different food production methods, each yielding promising results. Utilizing untapped city spaces, from rooftops to abandoned parking lots, these endeavors are shifting the urban food paradigm one harvest at a time.

5.1. The Sky is The Limit: Brooklyn Grange Farm, New York

On the rooftops of New York, urban agriculture has attained new heights, both figuratively and literally. Manhattan's skyline has always been synonymous with architectural marvels and twinkling city lights. Now, it is gradually becoming identified with a unique spectacle - lush green farms.

Brooklyn Grange Farm, boasting three rooftop locations in New York City, is one such gem in the urban landscape. Initiated in 2010, the farm occupies approximately 2.5 acres of rooftop space in Brooklyn and Queens, making it the world's largest soil rooftop farm. Over two million pounds of soil nourish a diverse myriad of crops, including peppers, leafy greens, tomatoes, eggplants, and several herbs.

The farming practices of Brooklyn Grange incorporate a comprehensive interaction with the urban ecosystem. The use of organic compost produced locally improves the soil fertility while reducing waste. Bees are employed purposefully, not only for honey but also for essential pollination. To conserve water, the farm collects rainwater, demonstrating an ideal circular economy in action.

5.2. A Desert Oasis: Agritopia, Arizona

Transitioning now to the Sonoran Desert's arid landscape, we discover Agritopia – a beautifully unique blend of urban living and agriculture in Gilbert, Arizona.

Agritopia occupies a 160-acre land parcel, featuring suburban homes, 15 acres of certified organic farmland, and several community gardens. The objective here is to create an integrated, supportive community where food is the central character. From growing to processing and consuming, Agritopia ensures that all food cycles are within arm's length.

Agritopia has become an urban farming model for other communities to emulate. Open spaces have made room for fruitful trees, grapevine bower over walkways, and in front yard gardens, residents cultivate their chosen crops under guidance from the farm staff. This system reinforces both social interactions and fosters a sense of communal well-being.

5.3. Urban Aquaponics: Sweet Water Organics, Milwaukee

Promising sustainable food production, aquaponics is a farming method that combines aquaculture (raising fish) and hydroponics (growing plants in water). Sweet Water Organics, based in Milwaukee, is a pioneer in this realm.

Situated within an old factory building, the farm leverages indoor spaces for its integrated fish and vegetable cultivation system. Tilapia and Yellow Perch are raised in large tanks, and their waste-rich water is used as a nutrient source for lettuce and other greens. After filtering by these plants, the water is recycled back to the fish tanks, creating a balanced, self-sustaining ecosystem.

Sweet Water Organics exemplifies the potential of adaptive reuse of urban spaces and resource recycling. Furthermore, an aquaponics system can be set up virtually anywhere there's a roof and a source of water, making it viable for numerous urban settings.

5.4. Wholesome Revitalization: Plant Chicago, Chicago

Plant Chicago is a non-profit organization based in the Back of the Yards neighborhood. From a vast icon of industrial production (a 93,500 sq ft former meatpacking plant), Plant Chicago has cultivated a thriving, collaborative community of small sustainable businesses, including farms, kombucha breweries and bakeries.

The concept of a "circular economy" is central to Plant Chicago's operations. Supporting a community of over a dozen small food businesses, Plant Chicago is a testament to the applied principles of waste-reduction and resource-efficiency. One business's waste becomes another's input. Therefore, the site has become a model of urban revitalization.

Championing urban farming as a viable solution requires an understanding of these novel and diverse models. Each bears unique lessons and shared confirmations of the potential of urban agriculture. Let these cases serve as blueprints, inspiration, and arguments for why the future of the cities may well be green. More than a trend, the urban food web movement brings vital ecological and social benefits and strengthens urban resilience.

Moving from concrete to cultivation doesn't only translate to improved food security, enhanced biodiversity, and better health; it is also an act of reclaiming the urban environment, one crop at a time.

Chapter 6. Resilience and Food Security: Embracing Local Autonomy

Urbanization is a double-edged sword: while it offers economic and social opportunities, it also exerts significant pressure on natural resources and food security. For many cities, this translates into an increased dependence on distant food sources, vulnerability to supply disruptions, and greater environmental impact due to food transport.

6.1. Embracing the Importance of Resilience

Resilience, in the context of Urban Food Webs, refers to the capacity of an urban ecosystem to maintain continuity of its food supply in the face of potential disruptions, including environmental, socioeconomic, or political crises.

Food security issues should not be viewed solely through the lens of 'producing more food'. Instead, it is essential to focus on enhancing the resilience of the food systems, making them adaptable and robust in turbulent conditions. Risk mitigation strategies, like creating buffers and advocating for redundancy in production and distribution channels, must be explored.

Enhancing urban resilience isn't just about surviving crises but also about making food systems more equitable by addressing existing inequities. Sustainable food systems emphasize not just sufficient production but the equitable distribution and accessibility of nutritious food.

6.2. The Pathway to Local Autonomy

The idea of local autonomy in the context of Urban Food Webs refers to the city's ability to independently grow and supply a significant proportion of its food requirements. It implies the local food production system is sustainable, resilient, and responsive to the specific needs and tastes of the urban inhabitants.

Transitioning to food autonomy presents numerous benefits, from enhanced food security and urban resilience, local economic stimulation, reduced environmental impacts to improved community health outcomes. However, it is essential to note that local autonomy doesn't mean complete self-sufficiency – instead, it's about self-determination where a community has an active say in their food supply.

Some strategies to attain food autonomy include:

- .Urban farming: Urban farmers convert abandoned spaces, rooftops, balconies, and even walls into productive locations. This not only maximizes existing urban spaces but also reduces the carbon footprint associated with transporting food from rural farms.

- .Peri-urban agriculture: Peri-urban farming involves food production in the zones at the boundaries of the city, preserving agricultural land against the pressure of urban sprawl and providing a continuous supply of fresh produce.

- .Indoor and vertical farming: These high-tech methods can grow produce year-round, irrespective of outdoor climatic conditions, improving the predictability of food availability.

- .Community gardening: Community gardens, where locals commune to grow food, have potential benefits beyond food production like creating social networks, fostering a sense of community, and instilling positive values of responsibility and pride among participants.

6.3. Cultivating a Culture of Local Consumption

Urban food autonomy is deeply tied to cultivating a culture of local consumption. Local food production can only be resilient if it has a robust local market. Hence, city-dwellers must be encouraged to participate actively in local food production and consumption, fostering a 'farm-to-fork' culture.

Policy and urban planning should encourage urban citizens to buy local through initiatives like farmer's markets, discounts on local produce, and 'locavore' education campaigns explaining the principles and benefits of eating locally grown food.

Promoting local consumption goes a step further in transforming dietary patterns from a high-energy input, processed food diet towards more plant-based, climate-friendly, and healthy diets.

6.4. Harnessing Technology for Sustainable Urban Farming

Technology can play a significant role in enabling local food autonomy. For instance, Hydroponic and Aquaponics systems can optimize water use and enhance productivity in a limited space, making them ideal for high-density urban settings.

Drones and other automation tools can ensure precision farming in urban farms. Accurate weather prediction models, advanced irrigation systems, and smart soil monitoring devices can mitigate risks and optimize the yield of urban farms.

Digital platforms can streamline the distribution of locally grown food, by connecting urban farms directly to consumers, restaurants, and suppliers, thereby shortening food miles and reducing food waste.

While technology offers substantial potential, it can express inequities within the urban system, if not adequately managed. Therefore, policymakers should ensure access to these technologies is equitable and doesn't further marginalize disadvantaged groups.

6.5. The Power of Policy

The transformation towards resilient and autonomous urban food webs requires effective policy and regulatory frameworks. Policies should support urban farming initiatives by addressing key challenges such as land availability, access to resources, and training.

Urban farming, local food production, and consumption should be incorporated into city master-plans. Tax incentives, zoning regulations favoring urban farming, and financial and technical support are few strategies.

Lastly, policy and planning should prioritize a participatory and inclusive approach, bringing farmers, consumers, policymakers, and other stakeholders to the table to create robust and locally relevant solutions.

In conclusion, by embracing resilience and food security, cities can catalyze a paradigm shift towards sustainable urban food systems. Through strategies like urban farming, local consumption, technology adoption, and effective policy, cities worldwide can promote local autonomy, thereby creating a resilient, healthy and sustainable urban ecosystem.

Chapter 7. The Benefits of Urban Food Webs: Physical and Socioeconomic

Urban Food Webs ripple with countless benefits, cascading across various domains such as physical health, socio-economic dynamics, environment, and communal connectivity. In essence, the advantages penetrate both the internal world of individuals reaping the direct benefits and influence the larger societal fabric that is positively tinkered with the enrichment of these sustainable practices.

7.1. Physical Health Benefits

Undeniably, one of the most significant aspects of Urban Food Webs is the fresh, nutrition-rich produce they bring forth. Shifting focus from highly processed, energy-dense, and nutrient-poor foods can drastically improve health outcomes. Here, we explore the multiple leafy dimensions of this transformation.

7.1.1. Nutrient Rich Produce

Urban Food Webs offer a consistent supply of fresh fruits, vegetables, herbs, and greens, which are critical to maintaining a balanced, nutrient-dense diet. Besides their vitamin, mineral, and dietary fiber contents that are crucial for overall well-being, these foods, being local and fresh, have a lesser likelihood of nutrient loss, which tends to occur during long transport times. This benefit must not be understated, especially in urban areas where access to quality produce may be limited due to distance, cost or availability.

7.1.2. Lower Obesity Risk

Having direct involvement in food production has also been linked with lower obesity rates. Increased physical activity associated with urban gardening and farming and the high consumption of fruits and vegetables foster a healthier lifestyle, thereby mitigating obesity and its related health issues like heart disease and diabetes.

7.2. Socioeconomic Benefits

One can't gloss over the socioeconomic impacts of Urban Food Webs. They have the potential to reform urban landscapes, economy, job opportunities, and income distribution, bringing about a positive paradigm shift.

7.2.1. Employment Opportunities

Urban Food Webs can function as job engines, providing opportunities for individuals to work in urban farming, distribution, or marketing. They can be especially catalytic in areas ridden with unemployment. Additionally, they offer a chance to acquire new skills, like farming and soil management or learning how to run a sustainable business.

7.2.2. Stimulation of Local Economy

By promoting a localized food system, money flows within the community instead of leaking to distant agribusiness. The result is an increased availability of funds for reinvestment within the urban confines. Furthermore, the self-sufficiency engendered can provide a shock absorber in times of economic instability or food price hikes.

7.3. Engendering Community Bonds

Urban Food Webs function as a social adhesive, bringing people together, enhancing community relationships, and bridging the gap between different generations and cultural backgrounds.

7.3.1. Building Community Connections

The act of jointly growing, harvesting, and sharing food enables community interactions and networks. Neighborhoods become more than places of residence; they transform into interactive, engaging environments, fostering friendships, and offering mutual support. The deepened sense of community can lead to increased safety and involvement.

7.4. Educational Opportunities

Urban Food Webs can be a living classroom, teaching children and adults alike about the importance of local food systems, nutrition, environmental preservation, agriculture, and entrepreneurship.

7.4.1. Rediscovering Food and Agriculture

Urban dwellers, particularly younger generations, often lack a connection with food and its origin. By integrating food production into urban life, Urban Food Webs can facilitate a whole new perspective on the role and importance of food and farming.

7.4.2. Promoting Sustainability

Urban Food Webs offer concrete ways to learn about sustainable practices, making the abstract concept of sustainability a tangible reality. They provide practicable demonstrations on conserving resources, composting, reducing waste, and maintaining soil fertility, and act as laboratories for future green innovations.

Urban Food Webs encompass much more than just food production. They build healthier residents, a more robust economy, a vibrant community connection, and a platform for continuous learning. They represent a form of urban resilience and are integral components of sustainable cities.

By cultivating our urban landscapes, we are not only nurturing plants but our overall urban well-being in extraordinary ways. Implementing Urban Food Webs in our cities may perhaps be one of the most overarching strategies to champion a resilient, sustainable future for generations to come. Hence, it is crucial that we seed this concept into planning policies and community engagement, and let it flourish throughout urban expanses worldwide.

Chapter 8. Community Engagement in Urban Food Webs

Our investigation into the concept of Urban Food Webs would be incomplete without exploring the vital role of community engagement. Indeed, it is the involvement and participation of local communities that brings life and meaning to the concept of a food web and it is here that we focus on how community engagement can aid in the development of robust urban food webs.

8.1. Importance of Community Engagement

Community engagement in the context of Urban Food Webs is not only about ensuring local food production. Rather, it stimulates a sense of ownership and responsibility among local dwellers, leading to the creation of resilient, self-sufficient, and community-oriented urban centers. It offers a forum for sharing knowledge and skills, encouraging dialogue, and fostering connections among different stakeholders involved in local food production.

The sense of community ownership that arises from such participation is often a powerful force that motivates individuals to adopt sustainable practices. It also results in numerous social benefits, including increased social capital, enhanced quality of life, and increased local economic development.

8.2. Mobilizing Communities for Urban Food Production

Building a successful Urban Food Web begins with mobilizing the community. Community-based organizations and individuals can play a critical role in promoting urban food production. Strategies to promote community engagement might include workshops, seminars, and hands-on training sessions offering basic gardening skills, composting techniques, the principles of permaculture design, and other critical skills.

Furthermore, making use of vacant lands for community gardening not only fosters a communal spirit but can also deliver significant environmental benefits. Additionally, engagement activities could also be centered around celebrating the harvest such as community potlucks where dishes are made from locally grown produce.

8.3. Integrating Urban Food Webs in Local School Curriculum

Schools are essential pillars in promoting community-wide understanding and participation in Urban Food Webs. Integrating urban food web concepts into the school curriculum can disseminate knowledge at an impressionable age, embed sustainability consciousness, and cultivate future citizens committed to local food production. Such educational initiatives can leverage practical gardening classes, scientific explorations of soil, plant life, and insects, or in-depth discussions about the role urban agriculture can play in tackling climate change.

Furthermore, school gardens can serve as living laboratories, providing children with the firsthand experience of planting, nurturing, and harvesting food. It also provides the valuable lesson of understanding the source of their food and appreciate the resources required to deliver a meal to the plate.

8.4. Collaborative Models & Community-led Initiatives

Community-led initiatives often hold strong potential in fostering vibrant Urban Food Webs. Models such as Community Supported Agriculture (CSA) offer mutual benefits by bringing together consumers and producers. In a CSA model, community members buy "shares" of a local farm's harvest in advance and then receive a portion of the crops as they're harvested.

In a similar vein, food cooperatives or co-ops can be instrumental in promoting local food production where people unite to meet their common nutritional needs and aspirations through jointly-owned and democratically-controlled enterprises.

Such collaborative initiatives create deep connections among community members, foster a sense of shared responsibility, and help sustain local food economies. They also profoundly reflect the underlying principles of an Urban Food Web– the interconnectedness of people and their food system.

8.5. Conclusion

Community engagement in Urban Food Webs is a multi-faceted component that highlights the essence of sustainability: it brings together economic, environmental, and social dimensions of city living into a holistic framework. More than just a desire, community engagement is a necessity, critical for growing Urban Food Webs into the life veins of our cities. By fostering local participation, teaching new generations, and supporting collaborative initiatives, we are a step closer to resilient, self-sustaining urban centers, proving that the power to make our cities more sustainable lies within the communities that inhabit them.

Chapter 9. Urban Food Webs and the Future of Climate Change

As climate challenges become increasingly acute, the need for dynamic, durable, and effective initiatives grows. This intertwining of urban landscapes with local food production – in other words, the creation of Urban Food Webs – shines as a beacon of hope in our struggle against climate change.

9.1. Grip of the Climate Crisis

Any discussion concerning the future is invariably tethered to the current defining environmental issue of our era - climate change. The Intergovernmental Panel on Climate Change (IPCC) has delivered stark warnings that a rise in global temperature beyond 1.5 degrees Celsius will have catastrophic implications for all forms of life on our planet. Cities, covering only 2% of the earth's surface but producing 70% of its carbon emissions, are on the frontline of this crisis, amplifying the need for intentional, purposeful urban planning that is conscious of this existential threat.

9.2. The Promise of Urban Food Webs

Urban Food Webs exemplify such informed planning. Essentially, these webs are clusters of interconnected relationships between multiple stakeholders working in urban food production. From individual city-dwelling gardeners to larger agricultural operations, beekeepers, foragers, solar-powered hydroponics, and aquaponic systems, they all are vital contributors to these complex webs. The webs, in turn, foster community cohesion and decrease carbon output by prioritizing local produce over long-distance imports.

Green urban spaces like community gardens and rooftop farms contribute significantly to reducing the city's heat island effect, enhance urban biodiversity, and sequester carbon while maintaining their primary function of food production.

Linking these green spaces in networks magnifies the benefits. These distributed networks of food production facilitate local circular economies by recycling organic waste into productive urban soils. They also create avenues for nutrient and energy cycling within the cityscape.

9.3. Building the Web: Stakeholders in Concert

Developing Urban Food Webs demands collaboration. Urban planners, municipalities, agroecologists, architects, community activists, and even innovative businesses must converge on this nexus and frame a cohesive strategy. By aligning their visions, resources, and actions, they can weave the intricate net of a locally grounded urban glocal food system.

Such collaborative efforts prove that integrated Urban Food Webs are not just theoretical concepts but realizable and crucial elements for the cities of tomorrow. A promising example is found in Detroit, where a grassroots urban farming movement has, in the shadow of industrial collapse, reclaimed the land. The city now boasts over 1,500 community gardens, helping to rejuvenate the local community both socioeconomically and environmentally.

Without proper governance and supportive policies, these positive efforts could be undermined. Thus, all actors, while playing their unique roles, must operate within a scaffold of forward-looking urban food policies.

9.4. The Economic Model: Local, Circular, and Resilient

We encapsulate the benefits of Urban Food Webs within an economic model: a truly local, circular, and resilient economy. Local food systems boost local economies, provide jobs, increase consumers' access to nutritious food, and inculcate a sense of community ownership.

The circular economy aspect originates from the sustainable utilization of resources. In Urban Food Webs, organic waste plays an integral role by serving as compost in urban farms, thereby recycling nutrients and creating robust soils. The goal is not only zero-waste systems but regenerative ones, that not only do no harm but do good - for the environment, and for us.

Resiliency is arguably the most significant facet of this economic model. The current food system, heavily reliant on transport, proves fragile in times of crisis. Climate change-induced disruptions to our transport infrastructure could lead to devastating food shortages. Urban Food Webs, by contrast, rely on local production and therefore prove less susceptible to such disruptions, adding a layer of security to the city's food supply.

9.5. Conclusion: Creating Cities of the Future

Urban Food Webs are about much more than just food. They are manifestations of a sustainable vision for urban living, gauging community cohesion, increasing biodiversity, combating climate change, and encouraging economic localization against the backdrop of an escalating global crisis.

Cities must reimagine themselves as patches in an expansive, vibrant, cross-pollinating urban garden, in which every individual and community is an integral part of the city's Urban Food Web. Interlacing the fabric of urban life with the vines of these webs may lead us, in a future threatened by climate change, towards greener pastures.

Paving the path toward effective Urban Food Webs is an investment in our cities' people and their future. This challenging but rewarding endeavor may well be a cornerstone in our collective fight against climate change, and towards a resilient, vibrant, and sustainable urban existence.

Chapter 10. Policy and Future Direction for Urban Food Webs

There is a growing recognition of the importance of urban food systems in policy and planning discourse. As cities grapple with climate change, economic inequality, and food insecurity, the potential of urban agriculture and the interwoven nature of food webs to address these pressing challenges is becoming increasingly clear. This chapter will explore the policy implications and future direction for Urban Food Webs, pointing the way towards more sustainable, equitable, and vibrant cities of the future.

10.1. Urban Food Webs: Policy Implications

The benefits of urban agriculture are diverse and profound, ranging from improved food security and access to healthier diets, to the creation of green jobs and mitigation of urban heat islands. However, the successful integration of urban farming into city landscapes requires thoughtful policy design and implementation. Flexibility, inclusivity, and responsiveness should be the guiding principles.

Urban food policies should endorse the use of vacant and underutilized land for urban agriculture. Incentivizing private landowners to lease or donate their underused land for agricultural use, or implementing programs that convert vacant public land into urban farms, could spur local food production.

Another key enabler of Urban Food Webs is zoning regulation. Zoning codes often unwittingly pose as obstacles to urban agriculture by limiting the types of agriculture permissible. Diligently revisiting and amending these codes can remove barriers and stimulate growth in urban agriculture.

Moreover, urban food policies need to go beyond just agriculture and look at the entire food web. Establishing citywide composting programs can help convert food waste into nurturing soil for urban farms. Similarly, encouraging businesses to reduce food waste can also make a significant contribution to food security and waste management.

10.2. Building Resilient and Sustainable Food Webs

Urban Food Webs are not a silver bullet for every city's problems, but with the right policy tools, they can contribute to creating more resilient and sustainable cities. Building these food webs requires a balance of short-term action plans and long-term policy commitments.

Short-term goals may aim at immediate food security and access improvements. Maybe this means establishing more community gardens in food-insecure neighborhoods or setting up farmers markets in areas with poor access to fresh produce.

Long-term visions require more extensive planning. They could involve integrating Urban Food Webs into city redevelopment plans, incorporating agricultural education into school curricula, or setting citywide targets for reducing food waste.

10.3. Ensuring Equitable Access

Equity is a fundamental consideration in the establishment of urban agriculture and food webs. In communities where some households experience poverty, joblessness, or other forms of marginalization, access to land for farming or even to quality food can be a challenge.

To alleviate these disparities, policy measures should not only sanction but encourage urban food activities in low-income neighborhoods. Initiatives like community gardens and garden education programs can be powerful tools for integrating marginalized communities into local food systems.

Furthermore, city councils and local cooperatives might consider establishing agricultural job training programs, particularly among underemployed populations, offering a pathway to employment while also bolstering the city's productive capacity.

10.4. Influencing the Future Direction of Urban Food Webs

Looking ahead, the future of Urban Food Webs hinges on continued research, education, advocacy, and trial-and-error experimentation.

Research on urban agriculture needs to be ongoing. New technologies, methodologies, and challenges arise constantly, and city planners must stay abreast of the latest developments. Research will provide the evidence base for policy development and decision-making, pointing the way towards the most effective and sustainable models for urban farming.

Education efforts are invaluable in fostering appreciation for, and understanding of, Urban Food Webs. Civil society organizations, educational institutions, and even urban farm operators themselves have roles to play in promoting the importance of local food systems to wider audiences.

Advocating for beneficial policies, funding, and regulations is of vital importance. Advocacy groups, city officials, and engaged citizens can all help to keep Urban Food Webs high on policy agendas.

Trial-and-error experimentation is essential, as well. Every city is unique, and what works in one place may not work in another. Urban Food Webs need to be responsive enough to adapt to these unique characteristics and challenges.

Through this multifaceted approach to policy and planning, cities can begin to unlock the full potential of Urban Food Webs, crafting vibrant tapestries of sustainability, resilience, and inclusivity. As urbanization continues to surge, the next global crisis might be just around the corner, but the opportunity for our urban spaces to rise to the challenges of the future has never been greater. And building robust Urban Food Webs can be a strategic card in this game.

More than an afterthought, they need to be woven into the fabric of urban planning and policy-making, ensuring that our cities can feed their people, offering access to nutritious, locally-produced food. From policy implications to future directions, the promise of Urban Food Webs is too compelling to ignore.

Chapter 11. The Road Ahead: Implementing a Successful Urban Food Web in Your City

Urban Food Webs propose an integrated approach to local food production, where community participation and natural systems can create a symbiotic relationship between city life and nature. Despite this promising premise, implementing Urban Food Webs isn't a simple notion. It requires skillful planning, community involvement, and efficient resource management. Let's explore how certain strategies can provide the pathways to weave such webs in our cities.

11.1. Nurturing the Concept of Community Gardens

The first step towards building an Urban Food Web is establishing community gardens. Community gardens encourage city dwellers to interact with their local ecosystem, promoting active participation in food production. Hosting workshops can help educate residents about organic farming practices, composting, water conservation. Involve local schools, colleges, and organizations to further foster a collective sense of responsibility towards local food production.

Community Garden Checklist

Permission from the local authority for setting up the garden.

The involvement of local community in the initiation

Organising educational workshops

Community volunteers for garden maintenance

Developing a rainwater harvesting system for water conservation

Community Garden Checklist

Establishing a composting unit

11.2. Promoting Urban Farming Innovations

Urban agriculture technologies like vertical farming, hydroponics, and aquaponics can transform concrete buildings into lush, fertile farms. Vertical farming is an ideal solution for space-constrained urban areas, allowing agricultural activities to be carried out in multilayered stacked structures. Hydroponics is a soil-less growing technique, using water-based nutrient solutions, helping to conserve soil resources. Aquaponics combines aquaculture with hydroponics in a symbiotic environment, reducing the need for external nutrients.

In promoting these innovations, city administrators can provide incentives for private building owners to establish such facilities. Implementing guidelines for using these technologies can ensure that urban farms contribute to the sustainability of the Urban Food Web without causing any collateral environmental damage.

Urban Farming Innovations

Vertical Farming

Hydroponics

Aquaponics

11.3. Incorporating Urban Food Webs into City Planning

Urban Food Webs should be an integral part of the city's future development plans. Planners and architects can account for urban farms and community gardens while conceptualizing new constructions. Retrofitting existing infrastructures to accommodate urban farming innovations can also be a powerful way to expand the Urban Food Web. Such considerations will ensure that cities do not merely grow, they bloom.

City Planning for Urban Food Webs

Incorporating farming space in construction plans

Retrofitting existing buildings for urban farming

Policy support for urban farms

11.4. Engaging the Youth

Young minds provide the energy and passion required to drive change. Thus, integrating Urban Food Webs into educational curriculums encourages them to not just understand the concept, but also to participate actively. Project-based learning that involves working on community gardens or urban farms can promote hands-on understanding of sustainable food production.

Engaging Youth in Urban Food Webs

Urban farming workshops at schools

Setting up school gardens

Introduction to urban farming technologies in syllabus

Project-based learning initiatives

11.5. Ensuring a Circular Economy

A circular economy in the context of an Urban Food Web means that all outputs are efficiently used, and waste is minimized. Emphasis should be placed on efficient water usage, recycling nutrients through composting, reducing food waste and energy conservation. These practices ensure limited resources are utilized comprehensively, making the food web sustainable over the long run.

Ensuring Circular Economy in Urban Food Webs

Efficient water usage

Nutrient recycling through composting

Reducing food waste

Energy conservation

The transformative potential of Urban Food Webs is considerable, but the road to set them up is challenging. However, with effective strategies, unyielding community involvement, and a robust plan in place, our cities can become the saviors of our future, harboring self-sustaining urban ecosystems. Be it the simple reassurance of locally grown food or environmental equilibrium that such food webs promise, it's a beneficial journey for the society and the planet alike. It's time to re-imagine our cities, not merely as densely populated settlements, but as thriving ecosystems where people and nature coexist symbiotically, fostering a resilient future. The road lies ahead; let's navigate towards a sustainable green world.

www.ingramcontent.com/pod-product-compliance
Lightning Source LLC
Chambersburg PA
CBHW071039260726
48661CB00007B/3061